DO IT YOURSELF

Saving Water

The Water Cycle

Buffy Silverman

Heinemann Library
Chicago, Illinois

Customer Service 888-454-2279
Visit our website at www.heinemannraintree.com

Designed by Richard Parker and Tinstar Design Ltd, www.tinstar.co.uk

Printed and bound in China by Leo Paper Group

12 11 10 09 08
10 9 8 7 6 5 4 3 2 1

Library of Congress Cataloging-in-Publication Data
Silverman, Buffy.
Saving water : the water cycle / Buffy Silverman.
   p. cm. -- (Do it yourself)
   Includes bibliographical references and index.
   ISBN 978-1-4329-1092-1 (hc) -- ISBN 978-1-4329-1108-9 (pb) 1. Hydrologic cycle--Juvenile literature. 2. Water conservation--Juvenile literature. I. Title.
   GB848.S55 2008
   551.48--dc22

                           2008008671

Acknowledgments
The publishers would like to thank the following for permission to reproduce photographs: ©Alamy pp. **10** (Donald Pye), **28** (Karin Duthie); ©Corbis pp. **4** (Royalty Free), **21** (Grafton Smith), **42–43** (Michael DeYoung); ©FLPA (Richard Becker) p. **26**; ©Getty Images pp. **7** (DK Stock), **13** (The Image Bank), **31** (The Image Bank), **35** (Photodisc); ©Photolibrary pp. **6** (Robin Smith), **9** (Photodisc), **11** (Australian Only), **19** (Nordic Photos), **32** (Robert Harding Travel/Liba Taylor), **40** (Creatas); ©Science Photo Library pp. **15** (David Nunuk), **17** (Dr Jeremy Burgess), **25** (Robert Brook), **27** (Robert Brook), **29** (Paul Rapson), **30** (Paul Rapson).

Cover photograph of a drop of water dripping from a tap reproduced with permission of ©Photolibrary (81A Productions).

Every effort has been made to contact copyright holders of any material reproduced in this book. Any omissions will be rectified in subsequent printings if notice is given to the publishers.

The publishers would like to thank Nicholas Lapthorn for his help in the preparation of this book.

Disclaimer
All the Internet addresses (URLs) given in this book were valid at the time of going to press. However, due to the dynamic nature of the Internet, some addresses may have changed, or sites may have changed or ceased to exist since publication. While the author and publishers regret any inconvenience this may cause readers, no responsibility for any such changes can be accepted by either the author or the publishers. It is recommended that adults supervise children on the Internet.

Contents

Any words appearing in the text in bold, **like this**, are explained in the glossary.

Our Watery Home

If you looked at Earth from outer space, you would see blue water. Oceans cover most of our planet—about 70 percent of it. Their average depth is about 12,200 feet (3,720 meters). Earth has an incredible volume of water—about 326 million trillion gallons (1.26 billion trillion liters)!

Water, water, everywhere

With all this water, how can a shortage of water occur? Why do you hear people reminding you to turn off the faucet and not waste water?

Most of the water on Earth is in the oceans, and ocean water is salty. People cannot drink salt water or use it to grow plants or to wash clothes or dishes. Power plants cannot run on salt water to make all the goods we depend on.

From outer space, Earth looks like a watery place.

Freshwater

Only 3 percent of the water on Earth is **freshwater** that is not salty water from the oceans. About two-thirds of that freshwater is frozen in polar **ice caps** and **glaciers**. Most of the rest of our freshwater is underground, beneath deep layers of rock. Water that is deep in the ground is called **groundwater**. It is stored in gravel and sand and can move through cracks in rocks. People dig holes underground, called **wells**, to get groundwater for drinking and watering crops.

A small amount of freshwater flows on the surface of Earth in rivers, streams, and lakes. The clouds in the sky are also made of water. There is water in the bodies of all plants and animals.

The water in you

Your body is 65 percent water. That means if you weighed 100 pounds (45.4 kilograms), 65 pounds (29.5 kilograms) of you would be water!

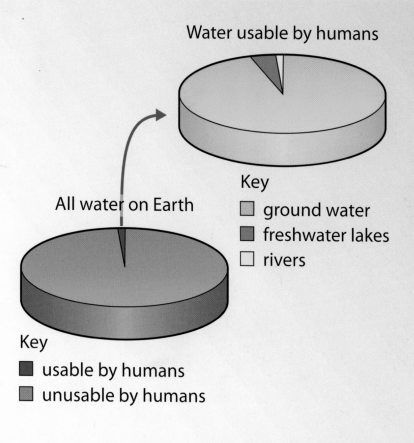

Water usable by humans

Key
- ☐ ground water
- ▨ freshwater lakes
- ☐ rivers

All water on Earth

Key
- ■ usable by humans
- ■ unusable by humans

People mostly depend on groundwater for survival.

How do you use water?

Every living thing on Earth needs water. People drink water to survive. To stay healthy, each person needs about 2.5 quarts (2.4 liters) of water each day. People get water from drinks and from food. A person can live without food for about a month, but can only survive without water for about one week.

Cities are often built near water.
Ships carry goods to and from a city.

Using water

People use water for cooking, washing, and bathing. An average person in the United States uses about 100 gallons (375 liters) of water each day.

People use water in ways that are not so obvious. People or goods may travel on water in boats. Many cities are built near water so goods can be shipped in and out.

People use water when they make things. For example, more than 39,000 gallons (148,000 liters) of water are used to manufacture one car. Power companies that make our heat and electricity also use a lot of water. Water is used to cool machines in factories. It is used to dissolve and carry material. It is boiled to make steam for running some machines.

Water helps keep people cool on a hot summer day.

Getting water

It is not always easy to get water. While some people simply turn on a faucet to get water, others have to carry all the water they need from a lake or stream. Would you use less water if you had to do this? When you know how important water is, you learn to use it wisely. By saving water, you help make sure there is enough fresh, clean water for the future.

The Water Cycle

Imagine a dinosaur drinking from a lake. The water that the dinosaur drank millions of years ago is the same water that you might drink today. Earth has a constant amount of water. The water we use today is the same water that was on Earth when life began.

The movement of water on Earth over time is known as the **water cycle**. Water continually moves through plants and animals. It moves around the planet.

Let's follow a drop of water on its journey, starting at the surface of a huge ocean. The sun shines on the ocean, heating the water. The **energy** from the sun drives the water cycle by making water **evaporate**. During this process, heat turns water to an invisible **gas** called water **vapor**. The vapor rises into the sky.

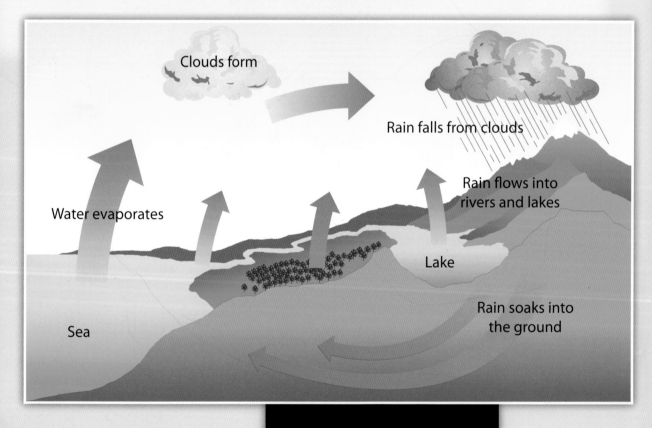

Clouds form

Rain falls from clouds

Rain flows into rivers and lakes

Water evaporates

Lake

Rain soaks into the ground

Sea

This diagram shows the water cycle.

Going up

As vapor rises higher in the sky, cooler temperatures turn it back to **liquid** water. This change from vapor to liquid is called **condensation**. Now the drop of water is part of a cloud, where it will stay for about 10 days. Winds blow the cloud over the land. As more and more drops **condense**, the cloud grows heavier and heavier. Finally, the drop of water falls to the earth as rain.

The drop of water lands in a **reservoir**, a human-made lake people use to store drinking water. It flows from there to a treatment plant, and then through a series of pipes until it reaches your home.

You turn on the faucet to brush your teeth. The drop of water splashes off your brush and goes down the drain. It flows out of your home and into a sewer. From the sewer it flows to a wastewater treatment plant, where it is cleaned. Eventually, the water drop evaporates again. The water cycle continues as the drop rises in the sky as water vapor.

Where does rain fall?

Some water that falls as rain or snow seeps underground. Plants and animals use some. Some joins rivers and lakes. Eventually, it journeys back to the sky to start the cycle over again.

Water's changing states

Water continuously travels through the water cycle. As it travels, water changes from the **state** of a gas to that of a liquid or **solid**. Water is special because it is the only substance on Earth that exists naturally as a gas, liquid, and solid.

A change in temperature causes water to change states. Water **freezes** at cold temperatures, turning from a liquid to a solid. If the temperature is 32° F (0° C) or below, liquid water turns to solid ice. As ice warms, it **melts** at 32° F (0° C) and changes back to liquid water. Water evaporates from liquid to gas when it is heated. As water vapor cools, it condenses back to liquid.

It is easy to observe solid and liquid water. Put ice cubes in a glass, and warm air causes them to melt. Place a tray of water in the freezer, and cold air turns it into ice.

When ice melts, it changes from a solid to a liquid.

Mist

Mist above a lake or mist from a pot of boiling water are not water vapor. They are simply tiny droplets of water suspended in the air.

Water vapor condenses on a cold glass.

Hidden vapor

Water vapor is invisible, but you can prove there is water vapor in the air around you. Fill a glass with ice and set it on a counter. The ice cools the glass. In a few minutes, the outside of the glass becomes wet. Where does this water come from? It comes from the air around the glass. Water vapor in the air condenses when the glass cools it. It turns to liquid water on the outside of the cold glass.

If you leave the glass out for a long time, the ice inside melts and changes to liquid water. The glass warms. Eventually water on the inside and outside of the glass will evaporate and become part of the water vapor in the surrounding air.

Changing density

For this activity you will need:

* A pitcher of water
* Food coloring
* An ice cube tray
* A glass
* Warm water
* Old clothing to wear when using food coloring

1 Add four drops of food coloring to a pitcher of water and gently mix it. Carefully fill an ice tray with the colored water and put it in the freezer. Leave it overnight.

2 When the cubes are frozen, fill a clear glass with warm water.

3 Put a colored cube in the water. Whether or not it sinks or floats depends on its **density**. Density is the weight of an object of a certain size. The ice will float if it is less dense than water. It will sink if it is more dense than water. Is ice more dense or less dense than water?

4 Watch the stream of colored water that melts from the ice cube. Does it float or sink? Is cold water more dense or less dense than the warm water around it? Is it more dense or less dense than the ice?

A closer look

Most substances get denser as they get colder. There are very few substances that are less dense as a solid than as a liquid. Water is one of them. Ice floats on top of water because ice is less dense than water.

However, when ice melts and turns into cold water, it becomes more dense than warm water. The colored water from the ice cube is colder than the surrounding water. It is more dense than warm water and sinks to the bottom of the glass. The colder the water, the more dense it is, until it reaches 39° F (4° C). Water starts to freeze below that temperature and expands and floats.

Life in a frozen pond

What happens to fish and other living things in a frozen pond in winter? The pond freezes on the surface. The water below the ice stays liquid. All winter, fish can swim below the ice. If water became denser as it froze, a pond would freeze solid!

People enjoy ice skating in the winter, when an ice rink will stay frozen.

The Water Cycle in Action

Steps to follow

Evaporation at work

For this activity you will need:
* A short drinking glass
* A large glass bowl
* Plastic wrap
* A large rubber band
* A small rock
* A notebook for recording observations

1 Create a model of the **water cycle** by placing a short drinking glass inside a large glass bowl. Fill the bowl with warm water, making sure that no water goes into the glass.

2 Cover the bowl with plastic wrap. Secure the cover with a large rubber band.

3 Place the rock on the plastic wrap, directly over the glass.

4 Carefully place the bowl in a sunny window.

5 Observe the bowl every half hour and record the changes that you see.

6 Return to the bowl the following day and record what you observe.

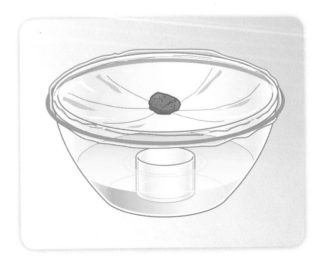

What is happening?

As the sun shines on your bowl, it warms the water inside. The water **evaporates** and turns to **vapor**. The sun also warms the air in the bowl. The vapor rises in the warm air. When the vapor reaches the plastic wrap, it **condenses**, turning to tiny droplets of water.

Because of the weight on the plastic wrap, the small droplets run down. They combine and form larger drops. As the drops increase in **density**, they fall from the plastic wrap and into the bowl.

You can also test how temperature changes the rate of evaporation. Set up two bowls, as before. Fill one with warm water, the other with ice water. Place both bowls next to each other on a sunny window.

Without evaporation, water could not cycle around Earth. About 90 percent of the water in the **atmosphere** comes from the evaporation of ocean water. **Energy** from the sun heats water on the ocean surface, and it evaporates.

Warm temperatures caused the water in this lake to evaporate, leaving dry land.

Water-saving tip

You can save water by reducing evaporation. Water your lawn and garden in the early morning or evening, when the sun is not shining. The water soaks into the ground before it evaporates.

Transpiration at work

For this activity you will need:

* A potted plant
* A plastic bag
* A twist tie
* A notebook for recording observations

1 You can prove that plants **transpire**, or give off water through their leaves. Ask an adult if you can borrow a potted plant with plenty of leaves.

2 Carefully place a plastic bag over a branch. Cover only the branch and leaves, not the soil. Close the bag around the branch with a twist tie. Be careful not to break off any leaves. Leave the plant on a sunny window.

3 Record your observations after an hour.

4 Continue to observe the plant for one day and take notes about what you see.

Warning: Always wash your hands after touching plants.

What is happening?

As you observe the plant, you should find water drops inside the bag. Where did the moisture come from? From your plant! The plant took in water from the soil through its roots. Water rose from the roots, through the stem, to the leaves. Extra water went out of the plant through the **stomata**, or **pores**, in the leaves. This process is called transpiration. The water became vapor in the warm air in the plastic bag. When the water vapor reached the plastic bag, it condensed, forming tiny droplets. When a plant transpires, it is similar to when an animal sweats.

Do plants transpire more when the sun shines? Repeat your experiment, using two potted plants. Try to use two plants that are the same kind and the same size. Cover the same number of leaves on both plants. Place one plant on a sunny window. Put the other plant in a dark closet. Compare the two plants in an hour and again the next day. How are they different?

A plant's stomata can be seen with a microscope.

Why is transpiration important?

Ninety percent of the water vapor on Earth comes from evaporation. The rest comes from plants. Trees take up huge amounts of water through their roots. They transpire excess water, and it becomes water vapor in the air. One oak tree can transpire 40,000 gallons (151,000 liters) of water per year.

Condensation at work

For this activity you will need:

* A wide-mouthed jar
* A small bowl that can sit in the opening of the jar
* Ice cubes
* A notebook for recording observations

1 Use the power of **condensation** to make a rainstorm. Carefully pour hot tap water into a wide-mouthed jar, filling it about halfway.

2 Set a small bowl on top of the jar and leave it for five minutes. During this time, water vapor will rise in the jar.

3 Fill the bowl with ice cubes, keeping it on the jar.

4 Observe the jar every 5 to 10 minutes for one hour. Record the changes you see. How long does it take before rain falls?

5 When you are finished observing, carefully lift the bowl and look underneath. Is rain still falling?

What is happening?

When you filled the jar with hot water, some of the water evaporated and rose. The vapor hit the ice-cold bowl, and it condensed into tiny droplets. As the droplets collided with each other, they grew and became heavier. Drops hung from the bowl until they became heavy enough to fall.

When water evaporates and transpires, it forms vapor in the air. Air currents carry water vapor high into the atmosphere. Air in the atmosphere is cooler than air close to the ground. As water vapor cools, it condenses into tiny droplets and forms clouds.

Water in clouds continually condenses and evaporates. Strong winds move clouds around Earth. The droplets in clouds condense on tiny specks of dust or smoke in the air. When **particles** collide, the droplets grow. Millions of cloud droplets are needed to produce one drop of rain.

During a storm a rain barrel collects rainwater, which can be used to water a garden.

Above Ground and Below

Steps to follow

How does water shape the land?

For this activity you will need:

* A half-gallon (2-liter) milk or juice carton
* Scissors
* Sand
* Rocks
* A plastic soda bottle

1 Place a milk carton on a table, with the spout facing up. With scissors, carefully cut out the top side of the carton. Do not cut the spout off, though.

2 Bring the carton outside. Lay it down on the ground, with the open side facing up. Fill it at least half full with sand. Pat the sand down.

3 Place a small rock or block of wood under the end without the spout. The end with the spout should be lower, so water can flow out.

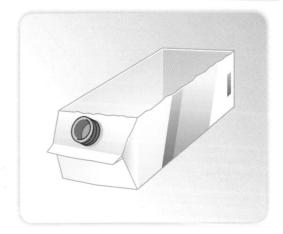

4 Fill a plastic soda bottle with water. Pour a steady stream of water slowly into the higher end of the carton.

5 Continue pouring water, and observe how the sand changes. Is the stream that forms straight or curving? Does its shape change as you pour more water?

6 Raise the end of the milk carton higher, propping it up with a larger rock or woodblock. Pour water again. How does the sand change this time?

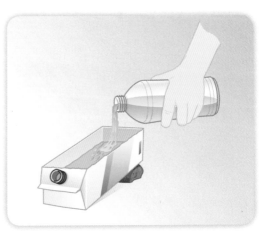

The power of water

The water you first poured formed a straight stream. As you poured more water, it wore away the sides of the stream, and the stream may have begun to curve. When you lifted the carton higher, the water came down with more force. It carved a deeper and deeper stream.

Over millions of years, river water cuts through rocks, making deep canyons.

Shaping the earth

Most rainwater that falls on land seeps underground. But some water stays on the surface. As water moves over the ground, it shapes the earth. It flows into streams and rivers. On its way to the ocean, water wears away land and changes it. Given enough time, water can wear away **solid** rock. It **erodes** tiny pieces of rock as it flows.

Water frozen in **glaciers** also shapes the land. It breaks up land as glaciers move and it carries huge boulders. Water also shapes beaches. Powerful waves pick up sand and deposit it elsewhere.

Steps to follow

Water underground

For this activity you will need:

* Three clear plastic cups (same size)
* A ruler
* A marker
* Sand
* Gravel (from a playground or aquarium gravel)
* A measuring cup
* A notebook for recording observations

1 With a ruler, measure down 1 inch (2.5 cm) from the top of three plastic cups and make a mark. Draw a line around each cup across the mark.

2 Fill one cup to the top with sand. Fill the second cup to the top with gravel. Fill the third cup with alternating layers of sand and gravel.

3 Measure 1 cup (240 ml) of water. Slowly add water to the sand **aquifer** until it is completely wet at the line you drew. This represents the level of the **water table**, or top level of **groundwater**. Record exactly how much water you poured into the cup.

4 Add water to the other two cups in the same way. Record the amount of water you poured into each.

What is happening?

When rain or snow falls to the ground, water seeps into the earth. Plant roots take up some of that water. But most of the water flows beneath the ground. It soaks through sand and soil. It seeps into cracks in rocks. This underground water is called groundwater.

Aquifers

An aquifer is an underground layer of rock or sand with water in it. Much of the water people drink or use for farming comes from aquifers. Your experiment shows how groundwater flows into an aquifer. Each cup represents an aquifer, an underground layer of rock or sand with water in it. Water flows into the **pore** spaces between every grain of sand and every piece of gravel. The amount of groundwater that an aquifer can hold depends on the size of these spaces. Because there is more space between pieces of gravel than between grains of sand, a gravel aquifer holds more groundwater. Water flows into larger spaces faster than it flows into small spaces.

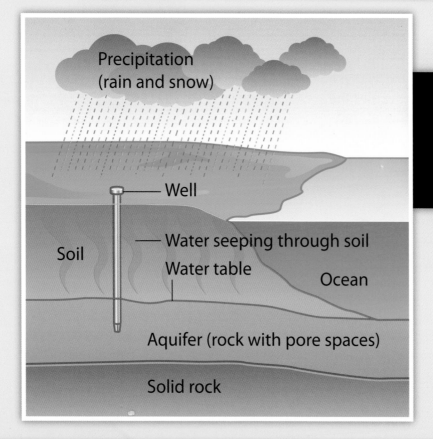

Water sinks farther down into the ground until it reaches a layer of hard rock with no pore spaces.

Groundwater pollution

For this activity you will need:

* A plastic cup
* Gravel
* Colored drink powder
* A plant mister or watering can

1 Fill a plastic cup almost to the top with gravel. Slowly pour in water until it is 1 inch (2.5 cm) below the surface of the gravel. This represents the level of the water table in an aquifer.

2 Sprinkle colored drink powder on top of the gravel. The colored drink powder represents **pollution**.

3 Spray water on the surface, as if it is raining. Watch how the rainwater carries the pollution underground. Where is the pollution greatest? How far does it trickle down?

Is your groundwater safe?

In the United States, there are more than 20,000 abandoned hazardous waste sites. The chemicals in these sites could leak into groundwater.

Poisonous chemicals are dumped on the ground. They can seep underground and mix with the groundwater.

Pollution's effects

Two-thirds of the **freshwater** available to people is groundwater. The other one-third is water that flows on the surface—in lakes, rivers, and streams. Most drinking water comes from groundwater. The crops that farmers grow are often watered with groundwater.

Because we depend on groundwater for drinking and farming, it is important to keep it clean. The colored drink powder that you sprinkled on the surface of your cup was carried through the model aquifer. In the same way, water from rain and snow carry **pollutants** underground.

In the winter, people put salt on roads so cars do not slide on ice. **Melting** snow washes the salt off of the road, and it soaks into the ground. Gasoline, used motor oil, **pesticides**, and other chemicals seep underground. Old storage tanks that hold chemicals can **corrode** and leak.

People try to store **hazardous waste** in safe places. But sometimes hazardous waste sites let pollutants into groundwater. Leaky barrels allow chemicals to seep into groundwater.

When groundwater is polluted, it is not safe for drinking and other human uses. Polluted water can make people and wildlife sick.

Protect your groundwater

You can help protect groundwater near your home so it is safe and clean. Here's how:

- Make a list of chemicals in your home that can harm groundwater. Paints, toilet bowl cleaners, drain cleaners, bleaches, rust removers, carpet cleaners, and some glues can harm groundwater. Pesticides and fertilizers for lawn and gardens can also harm groundwater. Label these chemicals by printing "DANGER: Groundwater Pollution" on labels. Stick a label on each bottle.

- Find out if your community has a hazardous waste collection day or a recycling center for chemical waste. Bring chemical wastes there.

- Encourage others to check labels and buy products that do not pollute water. Offer to clean the kitchen floor with a recipe that does not pollute: Mix 1 gallon (3.8 liters) of hot water with one-quarter cup (60 ml) of ammonia, one-quarter cup (60 ml) of vinegar, and 1 tablespoon (15 grams) of baking soda.

- Ask your family to limit the amount of fertilizers and pesticides they use. Offer to pick weeds in your garden instead of using chemicals. See if you can buy ladybugs or praying mantises to eat the bugs in your garden.

This ladybug feeds on tiny bugs called aphid.

Saving water and sinkholes

You help preserve groundwater when you save water. In some communities, groundwater is pumped out of an aquifer faster than rain and snow can replace it. When that happens, the level of the water table goes down.

Groundwater helps hold up the land. As the water table goes down, sinkholes can form. Near the coast, saltwater can move in when too much groundwater is pumped out. People cannot drink the salty water or use it for crops.

Many household products contain dangerous pollutants.

The Water You Drink

You turn on the faucet and water streams out. But where does that water come from before it reaches your home? Your water might be pumped out of the ground. Or it might be collected in a lake or **reservoir** during a rainfall.

These men are laying water pipes for pumping water underground.

Well water

If you live in a rural area, you probably have a **well** at your home. Many larger communities have large wells that pump **groundwater** for the entire community. The water passes through a treatment plant and then travels through pipes to homes.

Groundwater normally flows in the direction of **gravity**. When a well is drilled, a pump changes the flow of groundwater.

A hole is drilled through the ground, below the level of the **water table**. A metal pipe is dropped into the hole, which keeps the well from caving in. Groundwater moves into small openings in the well pipe or through the bottom of an open pipe. Until a pump is attached, the water just sits in the well.

Regularly testing water helps to keep it safe for drinking and farming.

A pump is attached to the bottom of a long pipe in the well. The pump uses electricity to pull out water. It connects to other pipes that bring water into a home or to a series of pipes for an entire community.

Groundwater is normally very clean. Groundwater seeps through dirt, sand, and gravel, filtering out **pollutants**. But, as we have seen, groundwater can become polluted from chemicals on the land.

Keep it clean

You can help keep well water clean. Rake away leaves and dirt from outside drains around your home. If your family uses a well, keep chemicals, paints, and motor oils away from it.

Water from reservoirs

If you live in a city or town, your water may not come from underground. Many communities rely on **surface water** that falls as rain or snow. The water is stored in a human-made lake called a reservoir. Before it travels through pipes to homes, it is cleaned and treated.

Before water reaches your home, it may be cleaned at a water treatment plant.

Your water

Find out where the water in your home and school come from. Do you have a well outside your home? Does your community pump up groundwater? Or does your city use a reservoir to hold surface water, and have a water treatment plant?

At a water treatment plant, the water is mixed with a chemical called alum. Dirt sticks to alum. The dirt clumps settle out in a basin. The water is then filtered through sand and gravel to clean it even more. Chlorine is added to kill bacteria and other germs. Fluoride is often added, too. The fluoride helps prevent cavities in teeth.

Water tower

Clean water is then pumped to a water tower. At the top of a water tower is a huge storage tank. A typical water tower tank holds about 50 times as much water as a swimming pool. Because the water tower is high above the ground, it puts the water under pressure. The pressure pushes water through water pipes all over the city.

Large pipes, called mains, carry water under city streets. Smaller pipes bring water into homes, schools, and other buildings. The pipes lead to the kitchens and bathrooms inside homes. When you turn on a faucet, the water flows out.

Water pipes

There are 1 million miles (1.6 million km) of water pipelines in the United States and Canada. That is enough pipe to circle Earth 40 times.

Water is pumped up to a water tower. From a tower, water has enough pressure to flow to pipes all through a town.

Saving Water Starts with You

We live on a planet that has more water covering it than land. Water moves around and around Earth. But people can use only about 1 percent of that water. In some countries, it is difficult for people to get clean water.

Will there always be enough **freshwater** for people? Will there be enough water to drink, to grow our food, and to make the goods we use? That depends on how we care for Earth's water.

Every day, people in some parts of the world must walk to find clean water and carry it to their homes.

The number of people in the world is growing. More and more people use more and more water. When people build new homes in new communities, they need water. Factories that make the goods that we rely on every day use water. Farmers use water to grow food. In some places people use water faster than **groundwater** can recharge or **reservoirs** refill.

When water becomes polluted, the problem grows. In the United States, unsafe groundwater has been found in all 50 states. About one in five people on Earth does not have access to clean water. Using unsafe water can make people sick.

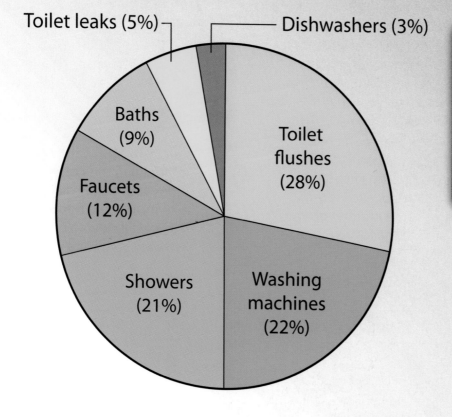

Household water consumption

Toilet leaks (5%) — Dishwashers (3%)

Baths (9%)

Faucets (12%)

Toilet flushes (28%)

Showers (21%)

Washing machines (22%)

Americans use about 75 to 80 gallons (280 to 300 liters) of water per day. The chart shows how that water is used.

Taking care of water

How can we help solve this problem? By keeping harmful chemicals away from groundwater, we make sure that our water stays clean. Each of us can also think of ways to use less water. Do you let water run down the drain while you soap your hands or brush your teeth? If you turn off the faucet, you will save water. Every day we send water down the drain.

In the United States, 5 percent of the water used in homes is lost from leaky toilets. There are many other ways people waste water. By learning how to **conserve** water, you can help make sure that there is enough water for the future.

How much water do you use?

For this activity you will need:

* Paper
* A pencil
* A calculator

1 Imagine a 1-gallon or a 1-liter jug. How many gallons or liters of water do you think your household uses every day?

2 Post a water chart to record water use in the bathroom, laundry room, and kitchen. Create a chart for each room that records the number of times each of the following are done:

4 Calculate your water use by multiplying the number of times your family did each activity. Use the figures in the chart below to help you estimate your total water use.

	Gallons per use	Number of uses	Gallons used
Bathroom			
Flush toilet	3 gallons		
Brush teeth	1 gallon		
Wash hands	1 gallon		
Shower	2 gallons/minute		
Bath	50 gallons		
Laundry Room			
Load of laundry	10 gallons/load		
Kitchen			
Run dishwasher	20 gallons/load		
Washing dishes by hand	5 gallons/load		

3 Ask your family to record each water use on the charts for three days.

5 Divide the total number of gallons by three to calculate your average daily use.

Other factors

How much water does your household use per day? Is it more or less than you expected?

The number of gallons you calculated does not include every water-using activity. You might also water the lawn, boil some noodles, or wash the dog. Newer toilets use fewer gallons per flush than older toilets. Newer homes have shower and faucet heads that use less water than older ones.

There are many uses for water in a typical household.

Stop that drip!

For this activity you will need:

* A measuring cup
* A calculator

1 Check for dripping faucets in your home or for faucets that are not shut all the way.

2 Put a measuring cup underneath a suspected leak. Collect and measure the amount of water that drips in one hour.

3 Multiply the amount that dripped by 24. That is how much water goes down the drain in a single day from the drip.

4 Multiply your daily total by seven. Your answer is the amount of water that the leaky faucet wastes in a week. How much is wasted in a year? Multiply your weekly total by 52 to find out.

5 Check all the faucets in your home for drips. Tell an adult if you find a drip and ask him or her to get a wrench and replace faucet washers.

How much do you save?

A tiny drip can waste 10 gallons (37.8 liters) every day. By fixing dripping faucets, you save water.

1 Remove the cover of the toilet tank and carefully set it aside.

2 Add a few drops of food coloring into the tank, so the water turns a deep color.

3 Wait 30 minutes and make sure no one uses the toilet.

4 If after 30 minutes any colored water has flowed into the toilet bowl, then you have a leak. Unless there is a leak, all of the colored water will stay in the tank until the toilet is flushed.

5 If you do suspect a leak, tell an adult. Cleaning the ball in the tank or replacing worn valves can fix some leaks.

A silent leak

You can often see and hear a dripping faucet, so you know to repair it. But a toilet leak is silent as it sends water to the sewer. A leaky toilet can waste 60 gallons (227 liters) of water in a day without anyone knowing it. Your family gets high water bills—and wastes water.

Warning: Ask an adult to help you with both of these activities.

Saving water when flushing

For this activity you will need:

* A half-gallon or 2-liter jug
* Gravel
* A calculator
* Rubber gloves

1 Most toilets use more water than needed for flushing. Ask an adult for permission to make your toilets use less water to flush.

2 Clean an empty half-gallon or 2-liter plastic jug.

3 Place a handful of gravel in the jug. The gravel acts as a weight to keep the jug upright.

4 Carefully remove the lid on the tank of the toilet.

5 Wearing rubber gloves, place the jug in the bottom of the toilet tank. Allow the jug to fill with water.

6 Replace the cover of the toilet tank.

How it works

When you flush, water stays inside the jug. The water in the jug does not empty, and the tank needs less water to refill. With each flush, you use less water. How much water does this save in a day? Multiply the number of flushes per day times the size of container you used. How much water do you save in one week?

Steps to follow

Saving water while brushing

For this activity you will need:

* A measuring cup
* A watch with a second hand
* A calculator
* A notebook for recording observations

1 Find an empty measuring cup. Turn the faucet on as you would if you were brushing your teeth. With your watch, determine the amount of time it takes to fill the measuring cup. Record your findings.

2 Time how long it takes you to brush your teeth. Divide the number of seconds you brush by the time it takes to fill the cup. This tells you the number of cups of water you use to brush your teeth.

3 Try changing how you brush. Wet your toothbrush and turn off the water. Brush your teeth. Turn on the water to rinse.

4 Time the number of seconds it takes to wet your brush and rinse. Divide this number by the time it takes to fill the cup. How much water do you now use to brush your teeth?

Warning: Ask an adult to help you with both of these activities.

Steps to follow

1 Write down all the ways you use water each day. Include the ways you use water in the bathroom, kitchen, and laundry room. List how you use water outside your home.

2 Look at each item on your list and think of ways your family can use less water. Make a list of five ways or more.

3 Share your list with your friends and family. Explain to your family why it is important to conserve water—so there will be enough clean water in the future.

Ways we use water

Turning off the water whilst brushing your teeth helps to conserve water.

Saving water

Here are some ideas to share with your family for conserving water:

- Don't run water to cool it every time you want a drink. Instead, keep a pitcher of water in the refrigerator.

- Check faucets for drips.

- Turn off the water while brushing your teeth.

- Use a kitchen timer when you shower. Set it for five minutes. Can you shorten your shower time even more? Try turning off the water while you soap your body. Your family can also buy a special head for the shower that saves water.

- Fill up the dishwasher completely before running it. Does your dishwasher have a water-saving setting? If so, use it.

- Only run the washing machine with a full load of laundry.

- Talk to your family about watering the lawn and garden. Don't water if it is going to rain. Water only in the early morning or evening so you don't lose water to **evaporation**.

- Plant native plants and plant varieties that don't need a lot of water.

- Put a layer of mulch around your trees and gardens to keep water from evaporating.

- Save water when you wash your car. Use a sponge and bucket instead of running water in a hose.

- Install a rain barrel to collect rainwater. Use the water in the barrel to water your garden.

- Record your water use in a notebook. Challenge yourself to find more ways that you and your family can save water.

Water for Today, Water for Tomorrow

Every day you use water in many ways. It cools you down when you swim on a hot summer day. You enjoy water when you paddle a canoe down a shady stream or catch fish in a quiet lake. In the winter, you may sled on snow-covered hills or build a snowman or a fort from snow. It is hard to imagine a world without enough water.

All living things depend on water. Trees and other plants take up water from the ground. Animals drink clean water or get water from their food. Fish and many other animals live and breathe underwater.

An important resource

Just like plants and animals, you cannot survive without water to drink. People also use water to keep clean and to grow food. Factories use water to make cars and toys. Power plants need water to make electricity and heat.

The water that we drink today is the same water that has gone through the **water cycle** around the world for millions and millions of years. Most of Earth is covered in water. However, there is only a small amount of **freshwater** that people can use. Without freshwater, we could not stay alive.

Sometimes people do not realize the importance of such limited water supplies. They may dump chemicals into the ground that seep into water and pollute it. They may waste water, thinking that they will always be able to turn on a faucet and get clean water.

Enough for all

The more you know about water, the more you understand its importance. You can help make sure there is enough water for the future by taking care of the water we have today. It is up to all of us to keep our water clean and to not waste water. If we use water wisely, there will be clean water in the future—for plants, for animals, and for us.

If we take care of water now, there will be clean water to enjoy in the future.

Glossary

aquifer underground layer of rock, sand, or gravel that contains water

atmosphere layer of gases that surround Earth

condensation process of changing from a gas to a liquid. Something that is condensed has gone through the process of condensation.

condense change from a gas to a liquid. For example, steam may condense on a window into water.

conserve use wisely. When we conserve resources, we are careful not to waste them.

corrode become destroyed by the action of water or chemicals

density weight of an object of a certain size. Something that is of a great weight is dense.

energy ability to make something happen. Energy can make things move or change shape.

erode wear away. Over many years, water can erode rock.

evaporate change from a liquid to a gas (vapor)

freeze change from a liquid to a solid when cold

freshwater water that does not contain salt

gas state of matter that spreads apart and fills any container. Water vapor is a gas.

glacier slowly moving mass of ice

gravity force by which all objects in the universe are attracted to one another

groundwater water held underground in spaces between rocks, sand, and soil

hazardous waste waste product from manufacturing that can harm people and the environment

ice cap permanent covering of ice over a large area, especially in the North or South Pole

liquid state of matter in which a substance flows easily, like water

melt process by which heat changes a substance from a solid to a liquid. When ice melts, it forms liquid water.

particle tiny part of something

pesticide chemical used to kill pests

pollutant unwanted substance that harms the environment—for example, sewage

pollution addition of unwanted substances that harm the environment. Things that cause pollution are pollutants.

pore small opening in the surface of a plant leaf. A pore is also a tiny hole that admits fluid. Water flows in the pores between sand grains.

reservoir lake used to store water for drinking. A reservoir can also be used to generate electricity.

solid state of a substance that has a definite size and shape

state condition. Substances exist as one of the three states of matter: solid, liquid, or gas.

stomata tiny openings in a leaf through which gases can pass

surface water water on Earth's surface. Surface water includes lakes, streams, rivers, and oceans.

transpire losing water vapor through leaves. Transpiration is the process through which plants transpire.

vapor gaseous form of a substance. Water vapor is what water in a gas state is called.

water cycle movement of water from the earth to the atmosphere and back to the earth

water table upper level of groundwater, below which spaces between particles are filled with water

well hole drilled into the ground to obtain water or other substances

Find Out More

Books

Barker, Charles Ferguson. *The Day the Great Lakes Drained Away*. Traverse City, Mich.: Mackinac Island, 2005.

This book gives an idea of what the lake floors of the Great Lakes would look like if all the water drained from them.

Kerley, Barbara. *A Cool Drink of Water*. Washington, D.C.: National Geographic Society, 2002.

This book explores how people all over the world collect and keep their drinking water cool.

Spilsbury, Louise. *Geography Focus: Running Water*. Chicago: Raintree, 2006.

This book looks at where the world's water supplies come from and how we use water.

Waldman, Neil. *The Snowflake: A Water Cycle Story*. Brookfield, Conn.: Millbrook, 2003.

This book follows the water cycle by looking at the journey of a single droplet of water.

Websites

Chesapeake Bay Foundation
www.cbf.org/site/DocServer/rain_barrel_guide-web.pdf?docID=2868
This website offers directions on how to build your own rain barrel.

EEK! Our Earth—Water Wonders
www.dnr.state.wi.us/org/caer/ce/eek/earth/groundwater/index.htm
Follow the path to cleaner water on this website.

Environmental Kids Club: Water
www.epa.gov/kids/water.htm
Play games, have fun, and learn about how to save water on the Environmental Protection Agency's kids' site.

WaterMatters.org Kids!
www.swfwmd.state.fl.us/education/kids/
Learn about the water cycle, hidden water, and more.